Fluttering Freedoms :

The Political Metamorphosis

<u>Preface</u>

This book isn't a collection of poems that complain. It also does not aim to provide concrete solutions. But, by tackling one problem at a time, I hope each poem triggers a series of thoughts and questions. These are issues which the world has forsaken. It has either been hidden or labelled unimportant. But just because something doesn't impact the West negatively, does not mean that none in the world suffer for it.

We are living in a world where we readily believe popular media. While we may be more informed with greater access to information and statistics, evidence and news is becoming increasingly easy to manipulate. While we cannot know for sure if our judgement is accurate, all I ask is to pause, and ponder perspectives from different angles. I ask to treat everyone with compassion for each of our background stories look vastly different.

Environmentalism, freedom, and justice are just a few words that come to us when we think about this new age in the 21st century. But what we stay unaware of are the cost behind everything. While we live under the pretence of cleaner atmospheres, there is someone else on the planet - toiling away under polluted and hazardous conditions. While we save our resources, wee are plundering someone else's. Fluttering Freedoms is a chance to liberate your mind. It is a chance to really start thinking.

<u>Index</u>

<u>***Free Seekers of Slaves***</u>

The land of the revolution,
Ironically poses a barrier,
To Africa's economic evolution,
And vows to keep it inferior.

From discrimination,
Lies too much to gain,
By exploitation,
Plunders and superiority they maintain.

Rouge et blanche et bleu,
Own half the foreign reserves,
Of a dozen African states and pursue,
Domination of natural mineral reserves.

The earthen jewels owe,
500 billion dollars annually,
To France alone,
While Britain, US, Russia and the world enter,
China has begun its debt trapping policies.

It serves multinational purposes,
To keep the downtrodden inferior,
Like how crony capitalism adores,
To keep the poor poor.

1

<u>The Scaly Olive Branch</u>

The gold and wooden
dancing figurines sit idle,
With blank stares, hidden,
Culture bleached and forgotten.

The snow with intent not stark,
Begins to extend,
a seemingly olive branch,
But the clouds of doom lark.

The people accept,
And celebrate,
As the olive branch twists and writhes,
And turns,
Into a snake.

Crimson Nile

The sand has slipped,
through generational fingers,
Yet the memory stings,
like the crimson river from a stabbing prick.

The thawing glaciers,
Always find a way,
Over the treasures of nature's,
Their will to sway.

Like a leeching parasite,
The mines again become iced,
Their own mine sites,
Snatched away before their eyes.

Still a slave
to snow,
That wondrously
survives their heat.

Remarkably,
This isn't history i'm talking about,
Rather a tale continuing endlessly,
Into today's present repent drought.

The fields of copper and riches,
Tremble under,
The rulers with vices,
From the lands faraway with blunder.

The bills too they don't allow,
To rest with their righteous owners,
The world watches upon clearly as stagnant pools now,
As the British and French tsunami incessantly poachers,
African treasuries,
And their stability.

<u>New Ages</u>

Multinational companies continue,
Their generational love to plunder,
In a form of slavery new,
Children still being used, uncorrected blunder.

The cobalt is hand-mined,
Even as companies have technology arsenals,
Alas, now the WHO is blind,
To the fatal fumes and particles.

As Congo struggles,
The country's children work hard to provide,
For mothers and families,
While their childhood and happiness have died.

We wake up every morning,
And the world is our oyster,
Brimming with freedom and opportunities,
But their dawn is a warning.

A warning to wake up,
And earn their $2.5 for 12 hours of labor,
This is our world corrupt,
Trapping toddlers under poverty's saber.

Monica is just four,
And she plays with rocks,
She sorts out minerals on the rock floor,
While we played with rocks in the playground and blocks.

7

Little buds exposed to life,
And life can't get harsher than this,
Can you imagine toddlers strive,
Just to combat hunger?

White Gold Rush

The dawn of the electric,
Signal the beginning of our cleaner greener world,
This is all a trick,
At our expense the third world suffers.

The big corporations put on a mask,
They say they help reduce carbon footprint,
But what of the billions of gallons of water they pump,
In the world's driest just to see the white gold glint?

The locals' environment concerns left unanswered,
As their resources are exploited,
And people enslaved,
For us to live greener.

Farmers to their own devices,
As rivers lay parched,
Their water redirected,
To the mining rises.

Land gets drier,
Brine leaves it infertile, worthless,
The desert's underground aquifer,
Is emptied,
The countries' climate change disaster,
Have been left no solutions, frenzied.

The Theatre of Wars

"And the decision of one man,
To launch a wholly unjustified,
And brutal invasion of Iraq, I mean Ukraine",
He falters, he laughs, he jokes, and continues,
"Iraq too… anyways",
He jested offhand.

With the petrodollar at stake,
And Saddam Hussein's challenge to US economy,
The Iraq attack was a perfect mistake,
While Bush hides behind,
The weapons of mass destruction façade.
(From when is "civilized bombing" okay?)

Wherever they vow
To bring down autocracy,
To peace endow,
They leave a bloody trail in the name of democracy,
And rip a nation apart.

We keep seeing this history repeated,
Yet nations stay silent,
After a few weeks of sensational headlines the press is defeated,
And truthsayers forced to be compliant.

We think we know,
The reality of situations,
But we are just watching a show,
Dramatically curated for us by nations and corporations.

All that we can do,
Is be kind to others,
Try to think without a bias view,
And don't let media and government,
Without analyzing,
influence you.

أجمل الدوريا دكتور

<u>Lurking Shadows of Influence</u>

The self-pronounced "influential" West leaders,
Blabber opinions on Oriental geopolitical issues,
They talk about peace, the West preachers,
Yet they love igniting borders, the West cheaters.

With flashy talks of human rights and equality,
They urge other countries to drop their arms,
And give up defending their polity,
Yet they forget their history of looting, of pillaging, of slavery.

They go even past borders,
Into the lands of socio-economic and environment policies,
In their path they create disorder,
Yet believe that they are the pinnacle of modern ideologies.

They've made the East
their trash and manufacturing processing facilities,
Then complain of the total waste beast,
Yet have they paused to look into their per capita waste
toxicities?

Venturing deeper into society,
We see detrimental influences in cultural gastronomy,
The combat against rising health issues comprises,
Of all traditions – natural and East that the West previously
chastises.

In the social realm a western influencer complains,
That the Qatar World Cup has gendered securities,
But from when has caring,
About female security,
Become a crime,
Against humanity?

It's time to wake up,
It's time to be proud of our roots,
For in whatever we do,
The West won't fail to criticize…
That's what an inferiority complex can do to you.

BIGTEK
7 NEWS
TONIGHT
TRUST

The Verdurous Betrayal

The world's dew glazed grass blades,
Sway and swarm the land of democracy,
The jades glisten with clear sanguine beads,
In the endless fields of futuristic prophecy.

The fields are optimistic,
To cover the world in leas,
From the desert of the Saharas,
To the Antarctic seas.

Yet they know not,
Of trees and secret weeds,
That from within cause rot,
And sow the destructive seeds.

The trees of governance,
Falsely shade waving flags of freedom,
As they allow wildflower and nitrogen fixers,
to thrive unchecked with the growing independence.

**Eroding Emeralds**

The wild purge the soil's nutrients,
The trees join in on the loot,
The green soldiers are patriots,
And helplessly believe that the trees will save their roots.

Unbeknownst to the emeralds,
Their trusty leaders defaulted,
A corroding community this heralds,
The word "democracy" is distorted.

We believe we are the owners of our money,
We believe we are the writers of our destiny,
We believe in a Constitution of free speech,
We fool ourselves into thinking we are in control.

The government and companies,
Deceive us into thinking they care,
ESGs are just another movement,
To capture market share.

Our government consorts with the depraved,
Under the allure of pure sapphire waterfalls,
Behind the roaring water of deception lies,
The two predators lounge over stolen riches and inhumane
political power grabs,
Safely protected by loopholes in their federal firewall.

Land of Dreams

A blooming white lily,
So sweet, so innocent,
Was robbed of her life's tranquility,
In the land of dreams, the Western world's pinnacle of freedom magnificent.

The States pride itself,
On being the heart of democracy and rights,
A place which denies liberty upon facing the abominable,
A place which unjustly defeated a 13 year old in her justice fight.

Even the unspeakable acts against young girls,
Do nothing to move lawmakers,
How do they expect her in life to move forward,
With a child - the abuser's living reminder?

The constitutional rights,
Do little to defend a woman,
The State shamelessly exercises control,
Over something as personal as her body.

Freedom over body choices notwithstanding,
The Roe v. Wade overturning has larger ripples,
Women fail to grapple with finances demanding,
And a life riddled with opportunities in cripples.

The reason the States' decision is especially frustrating,
Is because it was supposed to be the world's paragon of empowerment,
It endangers our forward movement, all feminist efforts straining,
The land of dreams is dead. It is up to us to continue campaigning.

I AM
A
"HUMAN"
FIRST

<u>*I am human first*</u>

24

Our first broken lens,
is gender,
But what happens when,
Race enters as a contender?

This race for equality,
Positions women of color as doubly handicapped,
Government policies filled with frivolity,
Under the guise of efficacy, they are trapped.

We are first seen,
As representations of the cultural stereotypes,
Then judged obscene,
And doubtfully for our worth,
Not as humans,
But questionably,
As a woman.

Paradoxical Perceptions

If I'm silent,
My brain is soft,

But if I'm defiant,
They say she must be stopped.

If I agree easily,
I am a prey to be manipulated,
But if I speak my thoughts openly,
Ugh, look at her, so opinionated.

If to everyone I'm smiling and warm,
I am inviting attention,
But if into my focused self I transform,
I am cold and distant in this world of defamation.

If i am assertive,
I am not confident, but bossy,
If I am focused,
I am not ambitious, I am selfish.

For similar actions,
They are considered studs,
But we are distractions,
We are called hoes.

If he takes care of family,
He is an amazing dad, husband, and son,
But if I perform the same activity,
It is ordinary, for it is my duty.

Who gave masculinity,
The positive connotation?
And made femininity,
An indisposition?

They do deal,
With mental health and other incapacities,
But we have suffered multiple times their ordeals,
Across generations ridden with no rights.

We are tired of this hypocrisy,
When will it end?

<u>Earth's Countless Raging Fires</u>

Unrest doesn't exist,
It is purposefully created,
Nations pitted against each other in the midst,
Of chaos inflated.

Countries breach borders,
And intellectually exacerbate,
Racial and dividing disorder,
Watching as others fall for the bait.

But everyone is concerned,
With everyone else,
While an outsider's backyard they burned,
They forgot to pay heed and helplessly watched,
As someone lit up their grass too.

In this governed world,
We are just pawns and puppets,
Around our eyes we have a blindfold furled,
We see only what we are allowed to see,
By media that's controlled,
By "true" democracies,
And influential companies.

Let us be free from hate,
Let us pause,
And take a moment to contemplate,
Why argue without a stake?
Instead be attentive,
To every time they try to fractionate,
For we believe only what we are shown,
So be kind and compassionate,
And attempt understanding,
Where everyone is coming from.

We are in this world together,
So to undo damage,
And breed the doves,
We must be benign to one another.

<u>Sources</u>

1. African Countries Still Pay $500B In Colonial Taxes To France Each Year (Peter Pedroncelli, The Moguldom Nation)
2. How France Continues to Dominate Its Former Colonies in Africa (Chris Dite, Jacobin)
3. African countries lost control to foreign mining companies – the 3 steps that allowed this to happen (Ben Radley, The Conversation)
4. Why France faces so much anger in West Africa (Paul Melly, BBC)
5. The True Cost of Lithium Mining (True Cost at Insider News, YouTube)
6. US left behind $7 billion of military equipment in Afghanistan after 2021 withdrawal, Pentagon report says (Ellie Kaufman, CNN)
7. U.S. secretly backing warlords in Somalia (Emily Wax and Karen DeYoung, NBC News)
8. CIA activities in Syria (Wikipedia)
9. Capitalisn't: Is 'Woke' Capitalism a Threat to Democracy? (Interview with Vivek Ramaswamy, Chicago Booth Review)
10. The real reasons Bush went to war (John Chapman, The Guardian)
11. The massive hypocrisy of the West's World Cup 'concerns' (Belén Fernández, Al Jazeera)
12. Roe v. Wade (Britannica)
13. How a 10-Year-Old Rape Victim Who Traveled for an Abortion Became Part of a Political Firestorm (Solcyré Burga, Time Magazine)
14. Tracking abortion laws across the United States (Carter Sherman and Andrew Witherspoon, The Guardian)
15. Inside the Congo cobalt mines that exploit children (Sky News YouTube)

-The end-